Rooted in Adoption Journal

Adoptee Writing Prompts for Self-Reflection, Discovery, and Healing

VERONICA BREAUX

DISCLAIMER

This journal allows you to reflect on your adoption experience through different writing prompts.

It is not meant as a substitute for direct expert assistance. If such a level of assistance is required, the services of a licensed mental health professional should be sought.

THOUGHTS OF SUICIDE

Help is available 24/7 at the National Suicide Prevention Hotline by calling 1-800-273-TALK (8255) or by visiting its website: www.suicidepreventionlifeline.org. Or you can text the word "HOME" to 741741 for free crisis counseling.

The writing prompts of this journal are not indicative of every adoptee's experience.

Table of Contents

Introduction

n 2019, I recruited friend, fellow adoptee, and filmmaker Shelby
Kilgore to assist me with the production of *Rooted in Adoption: A Collection
of Adoptee Reflections*. After its publication, I had no intention of pursuing
another book. Attempting to balance school and work amid other obliga-
tions, I did not believe it would be possible. It just goes to show that you never
know what life has in store for you. As someone with a career in mental health
care, I witness firsthand the seriousness that plagues the adoption community,
which is a shortage of trained adoption-competent professionals, limited
resources, and frequently a lack of empathy for adoptees, who are too often
misdiagnosed, dismissed, or told to be grateful.

Adoptees are at higher risk for suicide, mental illness, and are over-
represented in rehabilitation centers and prisons. With that in mind, I got to
work on my next project. Journal writing is one of the most popular forms
of self-expression. It allows us to privately externalize some of our innermost
and sometimes challenging thoughts. Adoptees are often silenced by the pro-
paganda of the expectation of the grateful adoptee, making it nearly impos-
sible to express genuine emotions without criticism from the rest of society.

Journals can serve as personal outlets for self-validation. The *Rooted
in Adoption Journal* is divided into seven sections: Love and Relationships,
Childhood Memories, Difficult Emotions, Listen to Adoptees, Adoption
and the Media, Search and Reunion, and Personal Growth. Expressing our
emotions can be emotionally draining. Often painful, intense memories that
we thought were deeply buried may once again resurface.

After each section, you will find a resting point with activities and tips,
reminding you to breathe and be gentle to yourself. The process of healing
is a journey and takes time. While you write, allow your thoughts to flow
onto the page freely. Do not be concerned with grammar, punctuation, or

awkward pauses that occur when explaining your adoption narrative to others. Just write from the heart, and most important, write unapologetically and write free. I sincerely hope that this journal will be a beneficial part of your path to recovery.

This Journal Belongs To . . .

Love
and
Relationships

"Loving ourselves
through the
process of owing
our story is the
bravest thing we
will ever do."

Brené Brown

Trauma can make you feel incapable of being loved. This is not uncommon for adoptees. The key to healing is learning how to love ourselves, even the parts that have been damaged. Describe any negative beliefs you have or have had in the past about yourself that may have prevented you from feeling loved. How did you change those beliefs? How can you change those beliefs now?

"Caring for your inner child has a powerful and surprisingly quick result: Do it and the child heals."

Martha Beck

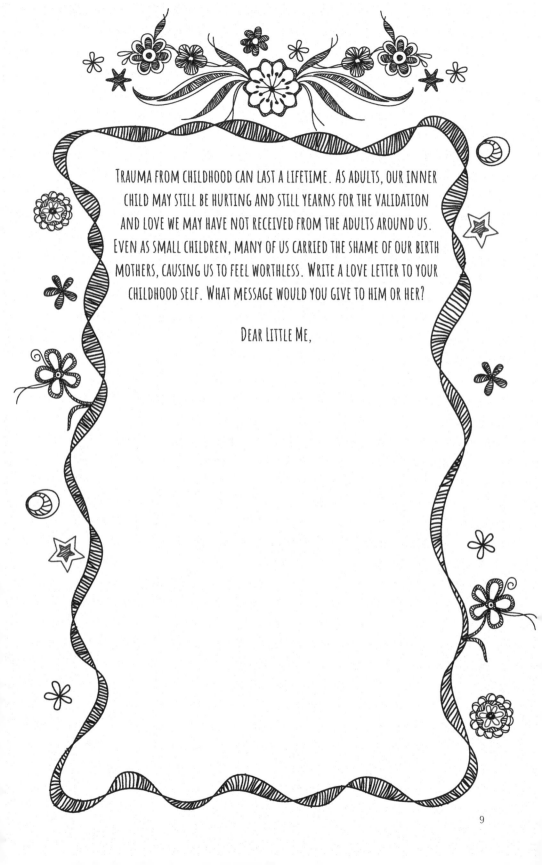

Trauma from childhood can last a lifetime. As adults, our inner child may still be hurting and still yearns for the validation and love we may have not received from the adults around us. Even as small children, many of us carried the shame of our birth mothers, causing us to feel worthless. Write a love letter to your childhood self. What message would you give to him or her?

Dear Little Me,

"I'm not afraid
of storms, for
I'm learning to
sail my ship."

Louisa May Alcott

Coming out of the fog is a redefining moment in an adoptee's life. While some of our family, friends, or peers will support us in our journey to healing, others may feel betrayed or hurt. Write about the defining moment that brought you out of the adoption fog. In what ways, has coming out of the fog affected the relationships you have had with your adoptive family or close friends?

"Love is a two-
way street
constantly under
construction."

Carroll Bryant

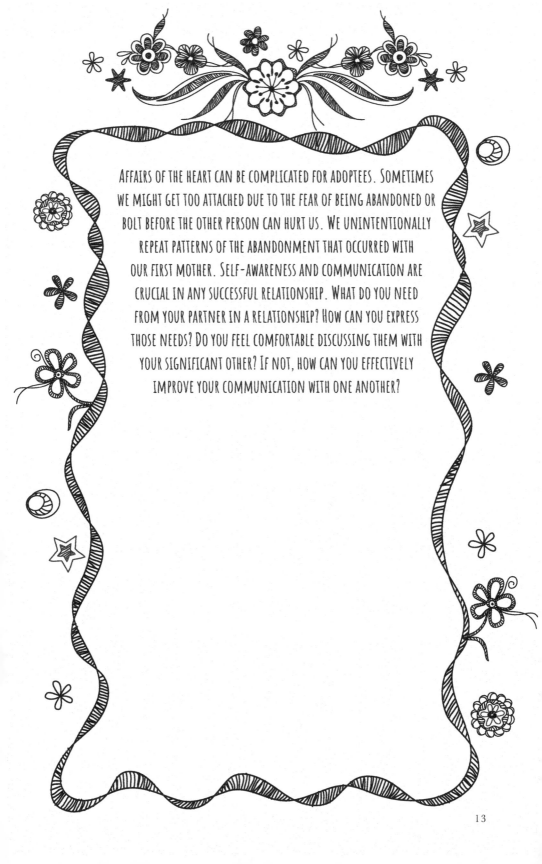

Affairs of the heart can be complicated for adoptees. Sometimes we might get too attached due to the fear of being abandoned or bolt before the other person can hurt us. We unintentionally repeat patterns of the abandonment that occurred with our first mother. Self-awareness and communication are crucial in any successful relationship. What do you need from your partner in a relationship? How can you express those needs? Do you feel comfortable discussing them with your significant other? If not, how can you effectively improve your communication with one another?

"You are not
required to set
yourself on fire to
keep other warm."

Unknown

14

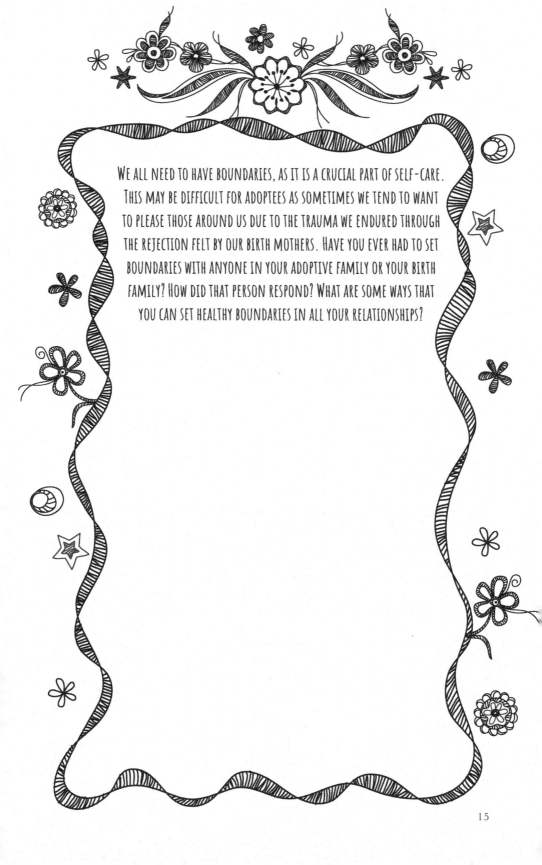

We all need to have boundaries, as it is a crucial part of self-care. This may be difficult for adoptees as sometimes we tend to want to please those around us due to the trauma we endured through the rejection felt by our birth mothers. Have you ever had to set boundaries with anyone in your adoptive family or your birth family? How did that person respond? What are some ways that you can set healthy boundaries in all your relationships?

"There are places
in the heart you
don't even know
exist until you
love a child."

Anne Lamott

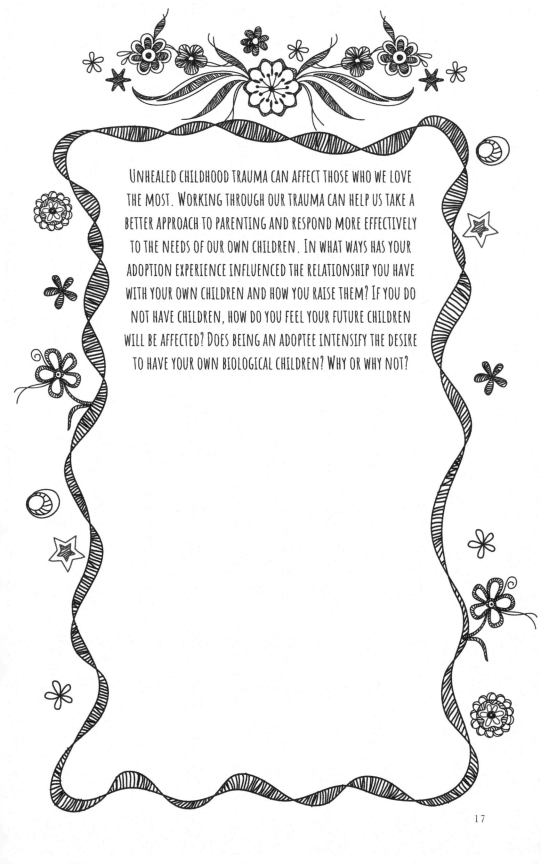

Unhealed childhood trauma can affect those who we love the most. Working through our trauma can help us take a better approach to parenting and respond more effectively to the needs of our own children. In what ways has your adoption experience influenced the relationship you have with your own children and how you raise them? If you do not have children, how do you feel your future children will be affected? Does being an adoptee intensify the desire to have your own biological children? Why or why not?

"Families are
the deepest
most screwed
up relationships
we have."

Antony Starr

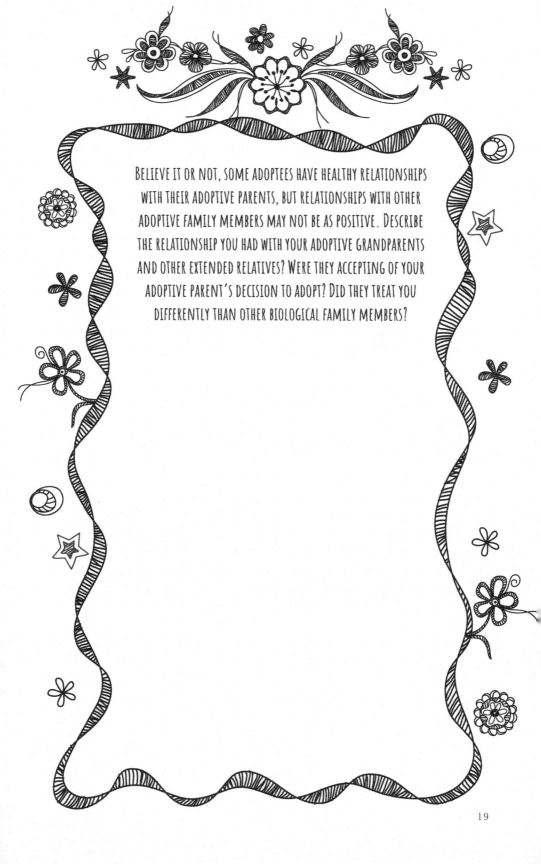

Believe it or not, some adoptees have healthy relationships with their adoptive parents, but relationships with other adoptive family members may not be as positive. Describe the relationship you had with your adoptive grandparents and other extended relatives? Were they accepting of your adoptive parent's decision to adopt? Did they treat you differently than other biological family members?

"The bond that links your true family is not one of blood, but of respect and joy in each other's life."

Richard Bach

Family is not necessarily related to us by blood. Family consists of relationships with those who love us and those who bring joy into our lives. Who are the people in your life who you consider family? Why do you consider those relationships as a significant part of your life?

Breathe Deeply

Today I feel..._____

because..._____

Self-care means taking care of yourself physically, mentally, spiritually, emotionally, and socially. Incorporating coping skills into your daily routine is one way to help maintain your mental well-being.

COPING SKILLS IDEA: POP SOME POPCORN, WATCH YOUR FAVORITE
MOVIE, OR BINGE WATCH YOUR FAVORITE TELEVISION SHOW.

Hydrate Often, Sleep Well, Eat Healthy

What can I do to take care of myself today?

_____

3 things that made me smile today:

_____

_____

_____

I Am Not My Experience

Today I am thankful for...

_____

Positive affirmations can help us manifest our goals or just make us feel good. On the next page, fill the jar with positive words to describe yourself, then color the picture. Start your affirmation with "I am…" and then include your positive word. Make your own affirmation jar at home by decorating an old jar with ribbons or photos and fill the inside with positive words or statements written on brightly colored strips of paper. Take out one affirmation each day and repeat it several times to yourself.

Childhood Memories

"Memory . . . is
the diary that
we all carry
about with us."

Oscar Wilde

DESCRIBE YOUR CHILDHOOD HOME.

"When there is an invisible elephant in the room, one is from time to time bound to trip over a trunk."

Karen Joy Fowler

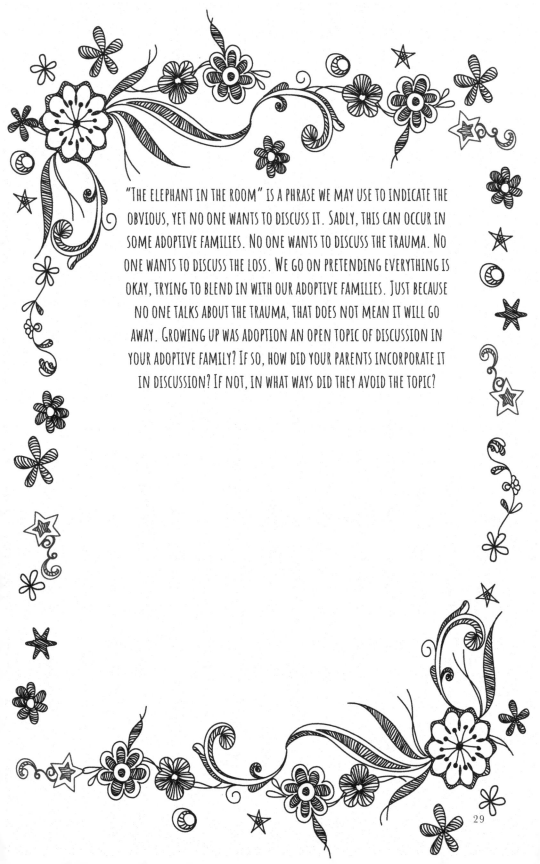

"The elephant in the room" is a phrase we may use to indicate the obvious, yet no one wants to discuss it. Sadly, this can occur in some adoptive families. No one wants to discuss the trauma. No one wants to discuss the loss. We go on pretending everything is okay, trying to blend in with our adoptive families. Just because no one talks about the trauma, that does not mean it will go away. Growing up was adoption an open topic of discussion in your adoptive family? If so, how did your parents incorporate it in discussion? If not, in what ways did they avoid the topic?

"There is no greater agony than bearing an untold story inside you."

Maya Angelou

The family tree is one of the first major assignments we encounter as children in school. Creating a family tree, writing an autobiography in English class, or studying genetics in biology can trigger many adoptees. Name some adoptee-related challenges you encountered in school from peers, teachers, or class assignments. How were you able to cope with those situations?

"Lies and secrets, they are like a cancer in the soul. They eat away what is good and leave only destruction behind."

Cassandra Clare

There used to be a time when professionals believed it was in the child's best interest not to conceal his or her adoption story. Even when adoptive parents choose to keep the adoption a secret, many adoptees say they sensed something did not feel right. How did you find out you were adopted? How did you respond? At what age did you truly understand the meaning of the word "adopted?"

"Fantasy is
hardly an escape
from reality.
it's a way of
understanding it."

Lloyd Alexander

Engaging in the realm of make-believe is typical for many small children. Many adoptees fantasize about their birth mother, especially those from closed adoptions, where even photographs are forbidden. As a child, did you ever fantasize about your birth mother? Describe your fantasies. Have you met your birth mother? How does your fantasy compare to the reality?

"Genes are like the story, and DNA is the language that the story is written in."

Sam Kean

Half of our DNA is inherited from our mother, and the other half is inherited from our father. We are a combination of the two, and often a likeliness of either one or both parents is handed down. When you were in school, did you ever notice how your friends slowly began to resemble their own biological parents while you had no genetic mirror of your own? How did it make you feel?

Breathe Deeply

Today I feel..._____

because..._____

Self-care means taking care of yourself physically, mentally, spiritually, emotionally, and socially. Incorporating coping skills into your daily routine is one way to help maintain your mental well-being.

COPING SKILLS IDEA: WRAP YOURSELF IN A SOFT BLANKET AND
DRINK A CUP OF YOUR FAVORITE HOT BEVERAGE.

Hydrate Often, Sleep Well, Eat Healthy

What can I do to take care of myself today?

_____

3 things that made me smile today:

_____

_____

_____

I Am Not My Experience

Today I am thankful for...

_____

On the next page, cut or tear pictures from old magazines or colorful pieces of paper to glue and make a collage of things that you remember from childhood.

Difficult Emotions

"Sometimes
the most
beautiful people
are beautifully
broken."

Robert M. Drake

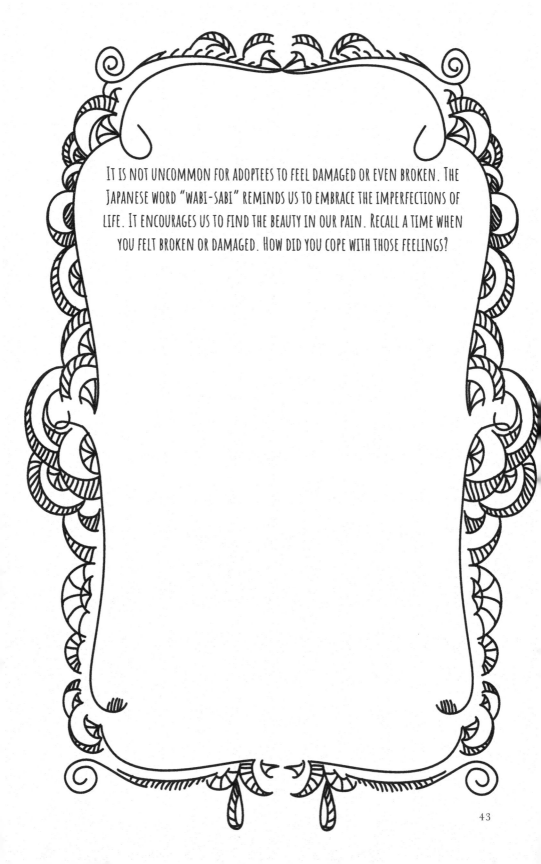

It is not uncommon for adoptees to feel damaged or even broken. The Japanese word "wabi-sabi" reminds us to embrace the imperfections of life. It encourages us to find the beauty in our pain. Recall a time when you felt broken or damaged. How did you cope with those feelings?

"The most
effective way to
destroy people
is to deny and
obliterate
their own
understanding of
their history."

George Orwell

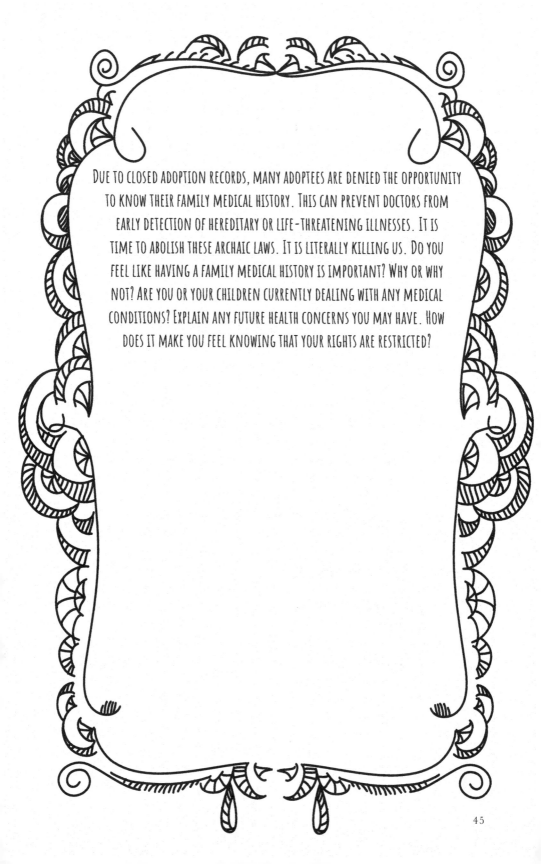

Due to closed adoption records, many adoptees are denied the opportunity to know their family medical history. This can prevent doctors from early detection of hereditary or life-threatening illnesses. It is time to abolish these archaic laws. It is literally killing us. Do you feel like having a family medical history is important? Why or why not? Are you or your children currently dealing with any medical conditions? Explain any future health concerns you may have. How does it make you feel knowing that your rights are restricted?

"Families are like branches on a tree. We grow in different directions, yet our roots remain as one."

Unknown

Genetic mirroring is when we see someone biologically related to us who shares the same physical traits. It is difficult for non-adoptees to comprehend the loss of genetic mirroring. Some adoptees experience this for the first time when they have their own biological children. Others may see it for the first time after meeting their birth families. Describe how you felt the first time you saw a family member who resembled you. What are some of the unique characteristics you share? What differences do you notice among you and your adoptive family members?

"If you want to
know who your
tribe is, speak
your truth. Then
see who sticks
around. Those are
the people who
get a spot in your
blanket fort."

Nanea Hoffman

Many adoptees mask their true feelings about their adoption experience from their adoptive parents and friends. We have fears of getting rejected or being dismissed. Have you ever spoken to your adoptive parents about your adoption experience? Why or why not? What happened when you finally revealed how you felt?

"Don't keep all
your feelings
sheltered—
express them.
Don't ever let
life shut you up."

Dr. Steve Maraboli

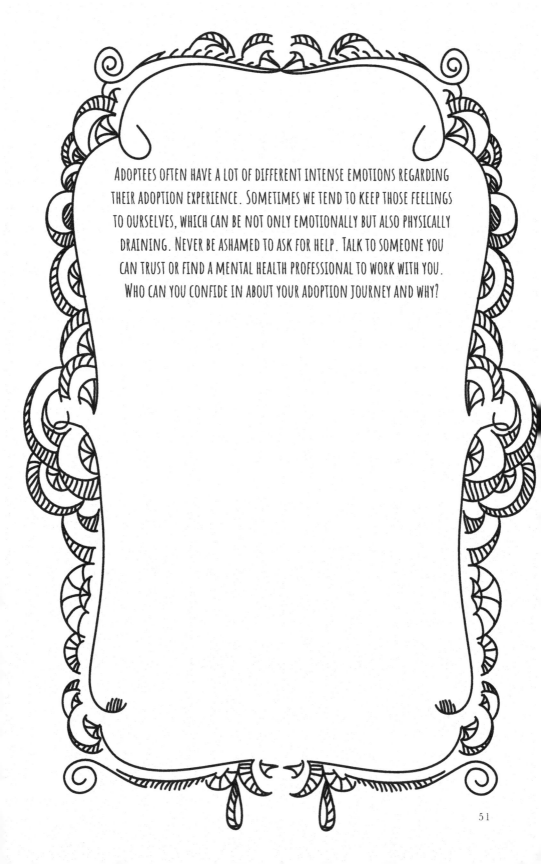

Adoptees often have a lot of different intense emotions regarding their adoption experience. Sometimes we tend to keep those feelings to ourselves, which can be not only emotionally but also physically draining. Never be ashamed to ask for help. Talk to someone you can trust or find a mental health professional to work with you. Who can you confide in about your adoption journey and why?

"Avoiding your triggers isn't healing. Healing happens when you're triggered and you're able to move through the pain, the pattern, and the story and walk your way to a different ending."

Vienna Pharaon

Trauma triggers can force us to relieve the abandonment and rejection of our adoption all over again. For some adoptees, a trigger may include birthdays, Mother's Day, the birth of a new family member, or the loss of an older family member. Being able to identify triggers can help you to manage the uncomfortable emotions that arise from them and put you in greater control. If you know it is going to rain, you should do your best to pack an umbrella. Identify situations that may trigger your adoption trauma. In what ways are you able to cope with those triggers?

"The walls we
build around us
to keep sadness
out also keeps
out the joy."

Jim Rohn

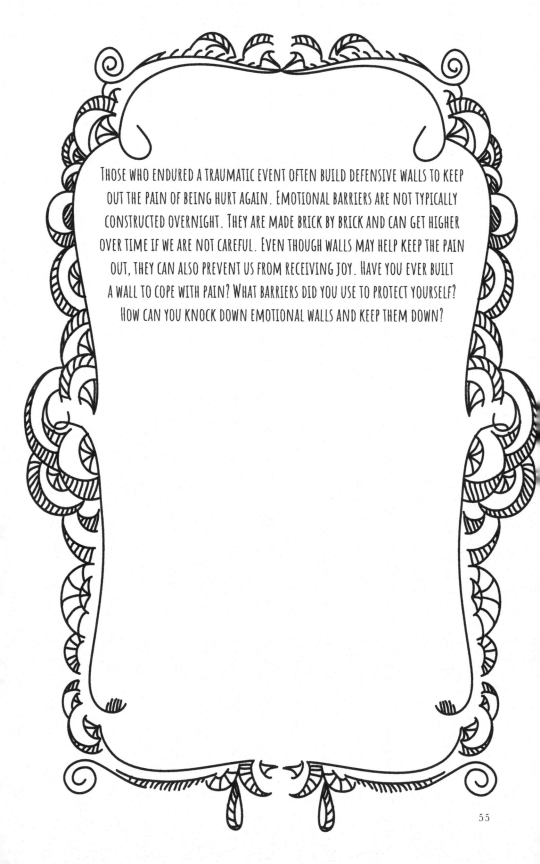

Those who endured a traumatic event often build defensive walls to keep out the pain of being hurt again. Emotional barriers are not typically constructed overnight. They are made brick by brick and can get higher over time if we are not careful. Even though walls may help keep the pain out, they can also prevent us from receiving joy. Have you ever built a wall to cope with pain? What barriers did you use to protect yourself? How can you knock down emotional walls and keep them down?

Happy Birthday!

BIRTHDAYS CAN BE PARTICULARLY DIFFICULT FOR ADOPTEES. A DAY THAT IS SUPPOSED TO SIGNIFY A MOMENTOUS OCCASION ONLY REMINDS ADOPTEES OF LOSS. IT IS IMPORTANT TO TAKE CARE OF OURSELVES ON THIS DAY AND SURROUND OURSELVES WITH THE PEOPLE WHO LOVE US. HOW DO YOU CELEBRATE BIRTHDAYS?

Happy Birth
Mother's Day!

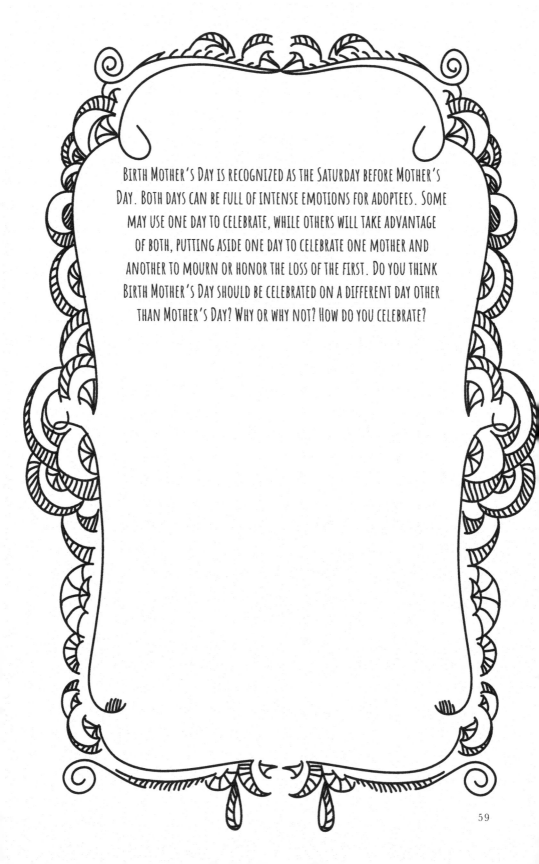

Birth Mother's Day is recognized as the Saturday before Mother's Day. Both days can be full of intense emotions for adoptees. Some may use one day to celebrate, while others will take advantage of both, putting aside one day to celebrate one mother and another to mourn or honor the loss of the first. Do you think Birth Mother's Day should be celebrated on a different day other than Mother's Day? Why or why not? How do you celebrate?

"When we recognize that someone is having [suicidal] thoughts, and we reach out, we are instantly planting a seed of hope that they're not invisible, that they're not alone."

Misty Vaughan Allen, Nevada Office of Suicide
Prevention Coordinator

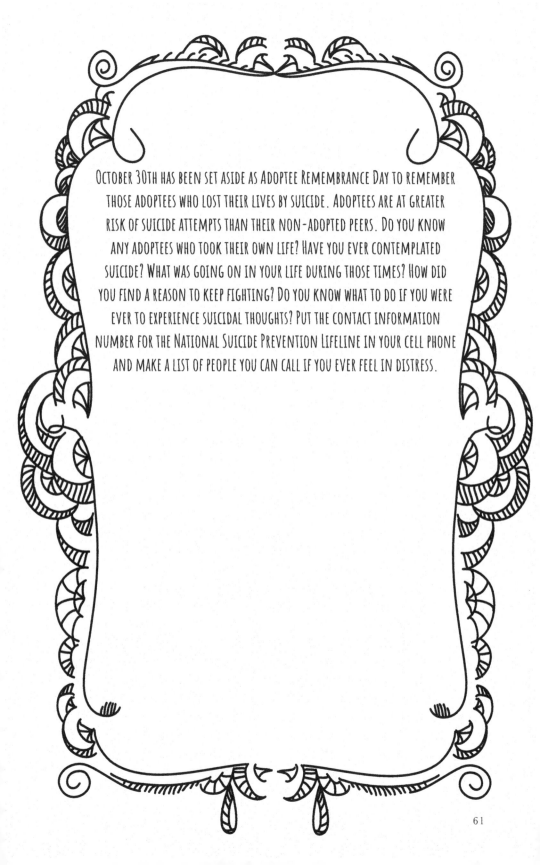

October 30th has been set aside as Adoptee Remembrance Day to remember those adoptees who lost their lives by suicide. Adoptees are at greater risk of suicide attempts than their non-adopted peers. Do you know any adoptees who took their own life? Have you ever contemplated suicide? What was going on in your life during those times? How did you find a reason to keep fighting? Do you know what to do if you were ever to experience suicidal thoughts? Put the contact information number for the National Suicide Prevention Lifeline in your cell phone and make a list of people you can call if you ever feel in distress.

"Grief is like the ocean; it comes in waves, ebbing and flowing. Sometimes the water is calm, and sometimes it is overwhelming. All we can do is learn to swim."

Vicki Harrison

LOSS DOES NOT ALWAYS INVOLVE A PHYSICAL DEATH, AND NO ONE IS MORE AWARE OF LOSS THAN ADOPTEES. IS IT MORE DIFFICULT FOR YOU TO COPE WITH LOSS THAN MOST PEOPLE YOU KNOW? THIS COULD INCLUDE LOSS OF A JOB, HEALTH, RELATIONSHIP, OR THE PHYSICAL PASSING OF SOMEONE YOU LOVE. HOW DO YOU HANDLE GRIEF?

"Everything has
a price. The price,
however, isn't
always money."

Ahmed Mostafa

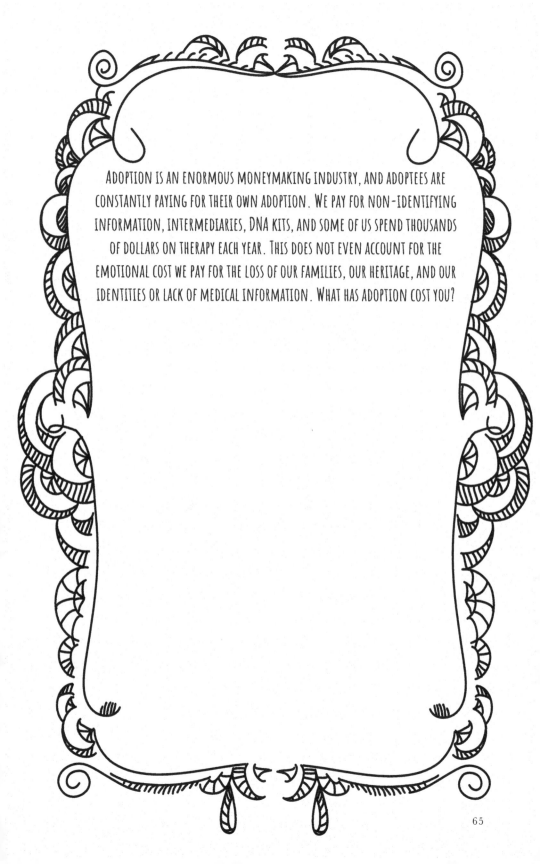

Adoption is an enormous moneymaking industry, and adoptees are constantly paying for their own adoption. We pay for non-identifying information, intermediaries, DNA kits, and some of us spend thousands of dollars on therapy each year. This does not even account for the emotional cost we pay for the loss of our families, our heritage, and our identities or lack of medical information. What has adoption cost you?

"Dreams express
what your soul
is telling you."

Eleni Gabre-Madhin

Themes of loss, rejection, or abandonment may cause disturbances in our sleep. Do you ever have dreams or nightmares related to adoption? If so, what are they about? Do you know what triggered them? Is there a reoccurring theme?

"Your hardest
times often lead
to the greatest
moments of
your life. Keep
going. Tough
situations build
strong people
in the end."

Roy T. Bennett

I AM HAVING A HARD TIME DEALING WITH . . .

"Our past shapes who we become, our experiences and things we go through. Things that scarred us and left their mark on our souls they drive our actions today."

Elena Vasilu

Adoptees are not born as blank slates. We are a combination of our upbringing as well as the genetic blueprint of our first families. In what ways do you think your life would have been different if you were raised with your birth family?

Breathe Deeply

Today I feel... _____

because... _____

Self-care means taking care of yourself physically, mentally, spiritually, emotionally, and socially. Incorporating coping skills into your daily routine is one way to help maintain your mental well-being.

COPING SKILLS IDEA: LIGHT YOUR FAVORITE SCENTED CANDLE AND MEDITATE.

Hydrate Often, Sleep Well, Eat Healthy

What can I do to take care of myself today?

_____

3 things that made me smile today:

_____

_____

_____

I Am Not My Experience

Today I am thankful for...

_____

Write your own personal self-care plan on the teacup, then color the picture on the next page.

YOU CAN'T POUR FROM AN EMPTY CUP

Listen
to Adoptees

"Debate and
divergence of
views can only
enrich our history
and culture."

Ibrahim Babangida

You are the debate team captain at your high school, and your team is headed to the state championship. The topic is "Do you think adoptees should receive access to their original birth certificate." Your team is defending the motion. Write a strong closing argument.

"if you are silent
about your pain,
they'll kill you
and say you
enjoyed it."

Zora Neale Hurston

You are chosen to give a seminar for adoptive parents titled, "Adoption as a Lifelong Journey." What three key points would you address in your lecture. You only have one hour, so make it count.

"Is there anyone
so wise as to learn
by the experience
of others?"

Voltaire

WHAT TOP THREE PIECES OF ADOPTEE WRITTEN LITERATURE WOULD YOU
SUGGEST TO AN ADOPTIVE PARENT? WHY WOULD YOU CHOOSE THOSE BOOKS?

"if you have knowledge, let others light their candle in it."

Margaret Fuller

You just met a mother who is considering making an adoption plan for her baby, and she asks if you will share your personal experience from an adoptee's perspective. Discuss your conversation.

"People say the most stupid things on the spur of the moment that they then have to retract."

Michael Palin

WHAT IS THE MOST INSANE THING ANYONE HAS EVER SAID TO YOU
ABOUT ADOPTION? HOW DID YOU RESPOND? WHAT WAS THEIR REACTION?
WOULD YOU RESPOND DIFFERENTLY TODAY? WHY OR WHY NOT?

"Sometimes it takes an expert to point out the obvious."

Scott Allen

No one is more qualified to speak on the adoption experience than adoptees. We are the experts. Based on your experience within your own adoptive family, what questions, precautions, and criteria would you advise adoption agencies to utilize when screening or choosing prospective adoptive parents?

Breathe Deeply

Today I feel..._____

because..._____

Self-care means taking care of yourself physically, mentally, spiritually, emotionally, and socially. Incorporating coping skills into your daily routine is one way to help maintain your mental well-being.

COPING SKILLS IDEA: CALL AN OLD FRIEND AND CATCH UP.

Hydrate Often, Sleep Well, Eat Healthy

What can I do to take care of myself today?

_____

3 things that made me smile today:

_____

_____

_____

I Am Not My Experience

Today I am thankful for...

_____

You are marching for adoptee rights. On the next page, write messages on the protest signs and then color the picture.

Adoption and the Media

"The most
honest form of
filmmaking is
to make a film
for yourself."

Peter Jackson

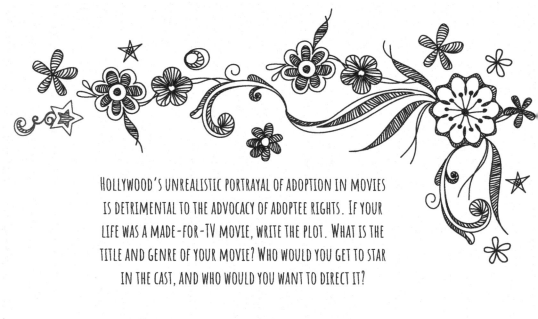

Hollywood's unrealistic portrayal of adoption in movies is detrimental to the advocacy of adoptee rights. If your life was a made-for-TV movie, write the plot. What is the title and genre of your movie? Who would you get to star in the cast, and who would you want to direct it?

"Music is the
emotional life
of most people."

Leonard Cohen

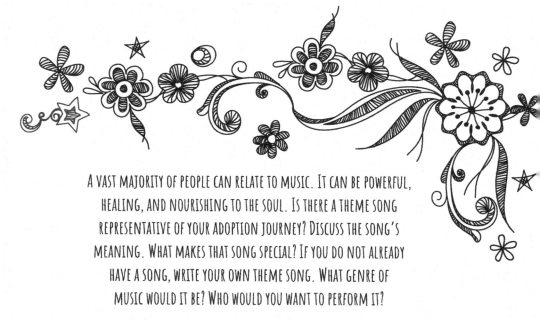

A VAST MAJORITY OF PEOPLE CAN RELATE TO MUSIC. IT CAN BE POWERFUL, HEALING, AND NOURISHING TO THE SOUL. IS THERE A THEME SONG REPRESENTATIVE OF YOUR ADOPTION JOURNEY? DISCUSS THE SONG'S MEANING. WHAT MAKES THAT SONG SPECIAL? IF YOU DO NOT ALREADY HAVE A SONG, WRITE YOUR OWN THEME SONG. WHAT GENRE OF MUSIC WOULD IT BE? WHO WOULD YOU WANT TO PERFORM IT?

"A podcast is
a great way
to develop
relationships
with hard-to-
reach people."

Tim Paige

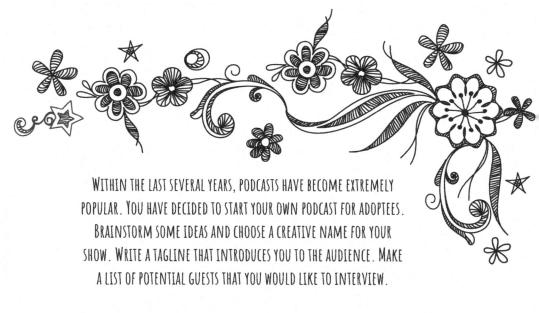

Within the last several years, podcasts have become extremely popular. You have decided to start your own podcast for adoptees. Brainstorm some ideas and choose a creative name for your show. Write a tagline that introduces you to the audience. Make a list of potential guests that you would like to interview.

"You cannot
open a book
without learning
something."

Confucius

The first adoption book I purchased was *The Primal Wound* by Nancy Verrier. It was terrifying and breathtaking all at the same time. It opened my eyes to the extent of trauma I had endured from the separation of my first mother and validated what I had been experiencing my entire life. What was the first book that you read on adoption? What books have been the most beneficial in your healing journey? Name a book that opened your eyes to a whole brand-new perspective on adoption. What did it teach you?

Breathe Deeply

Today I feel..._____

because..._____

Self-care means taking care of yourself physically, mentally, spiritually, emotionally, and socially. Incorporating coping skills into your daily routine is one way to help maintain your mental well-being.

COPING SKILLS IDEA: MAKE A VISION BOARD.

Hydrate Often, Sleep Well, Eat Healthy

What can I do to take care of myself today?

_____

3 things that made me smile today:

_____

_____

_____

I Am Not My Experience

Today I am thankful for...

_____

Subscribe to Shelby Redfield Kilgore's channel on YouTube, then color the picture on the next page.

ADOPTION EDUCATION

with shelby

REDFIELD Kilgore

SUBSCRIBE

Search
and Reunion

retrouvaille

(n.) the joy
of meeting or
finding someone
again after a
long separation,
rediscovery.

Pronunciation
re-tru-'vi

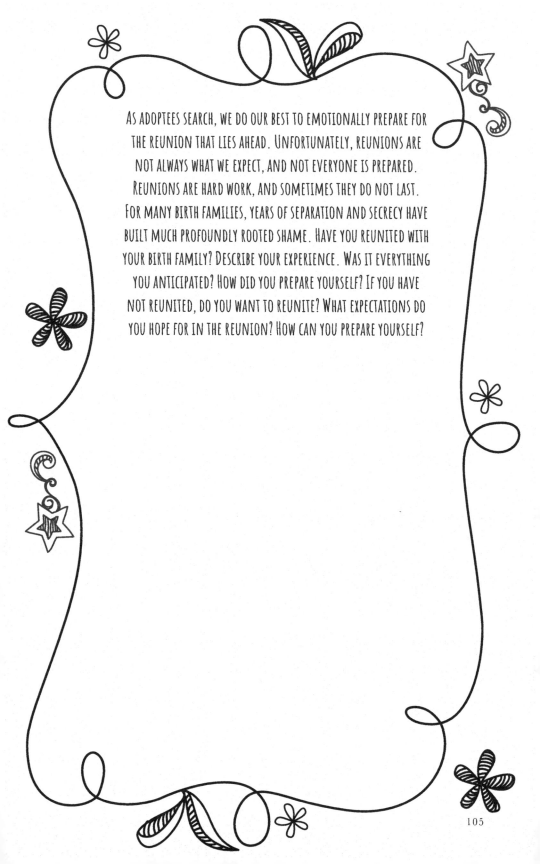

As adoptees search, we do our best to emotionally prepare for the reunion that lies ahead. Unfortunately, reunions are not always what we expect, and not everyone is prepared. Reunions are hard work, and sometimes they do not last. For many birth families, years of separation and secrecy have built much profoundly rooted shame. Have you reunited with your birth family? Describe your experience. Was it everything you anticipated? How did you prepare yourself? If you have not reunited, do you want to reunite? What expectations do you hope for in the reunion? How can you prepare yourself?

"Advice is what
we ask for when
we already know
the answer but
wish we didn't."

Erica Jong

A BIRTH MOTHER TELLS YOU THAT AFTER SEVERAL YEARS OF SEARCHING, SHE HAS FINALLY LOCATED HER OLDEST CHILD, WHOM SHE PLACED FOR ADOPTION WHEN SHE WAS EIGHTEEN YEARS OLD. TODAY HER CHILD IS TWENTY-ONE YEARS OLD. SHE TELLS YOU THAT SHE IS CURRENTLY MARRIED TO HER FIRST CHILD'S FATHER WITH THREE OTHER CHILDREN, WHOM SHE RAISED. SHE REPORTS SHE WANTS TO REUNITE WITH HER CHILD AND ASKS YOU THE BEST WAY TO PROCEED IN THIS SITUATION. WHAT ADVICE DO YOU GIVE HER?

"All truths
are easy to
understand
once they are
discovered;
the point is to
discover them."

Galileo Galilei

Even after reuniting with our birth families, laws prohibit most adoptees from receiving access to our own records. Do you have your original birth certificate? What did it feel like when you first held it in your hands? If you still do not have your original birth certificate, what steps have you taken toward getting it? What are the laws in your state regarding birth records for adopted adults? Has your birth family been instrumental in supporting your access to these records?

"There's a story behind everything . . . but behind all your stories is always your mother's story . . . because hers is where yours begins."

Mitch Albom

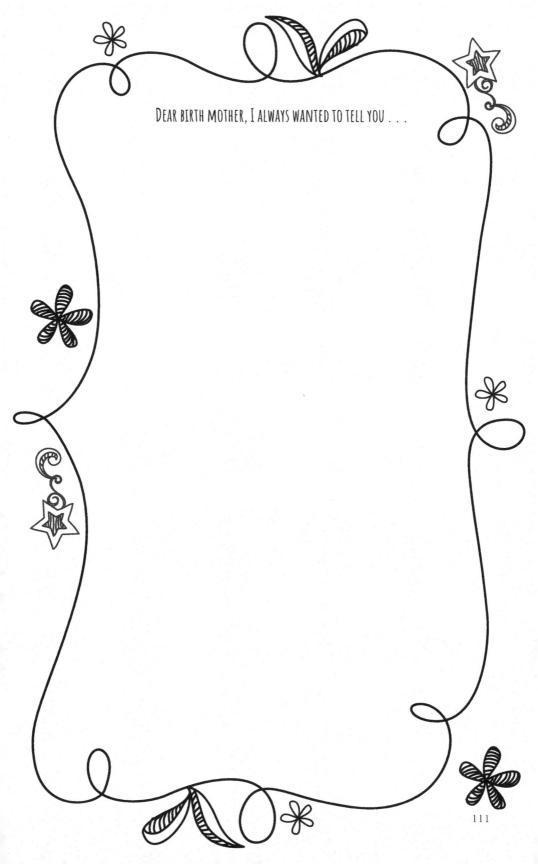

Dear birth mother, I always wanted to tell you . . .

111

"You don't know
who is important
to you until
you actually
lose them."

Mahatma Gandhi

Your adoption search has finally come to an end, and you have reunited with your birth mother and the rest of your birth family. To celebrate, you decide to get a tattoo to represent your adoption journey. Describe the sketch you would give your tattoo artist. What does it symbolize for you? Draw your design in the space below.

"One of the
most important
relationships
we have is the
relationship with
our mothers."

Iyanla Vanzant

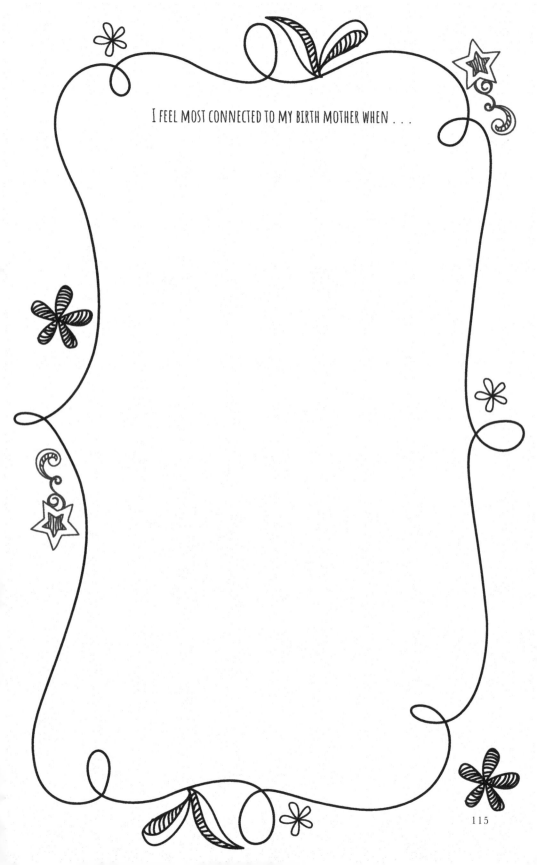

I FEEL MOST CONNECTED TO MY BIRTH MOTHER WHEN . . .

"Maybe you are
searching among
the branches, for
what only appears
in the roots."

Rumi

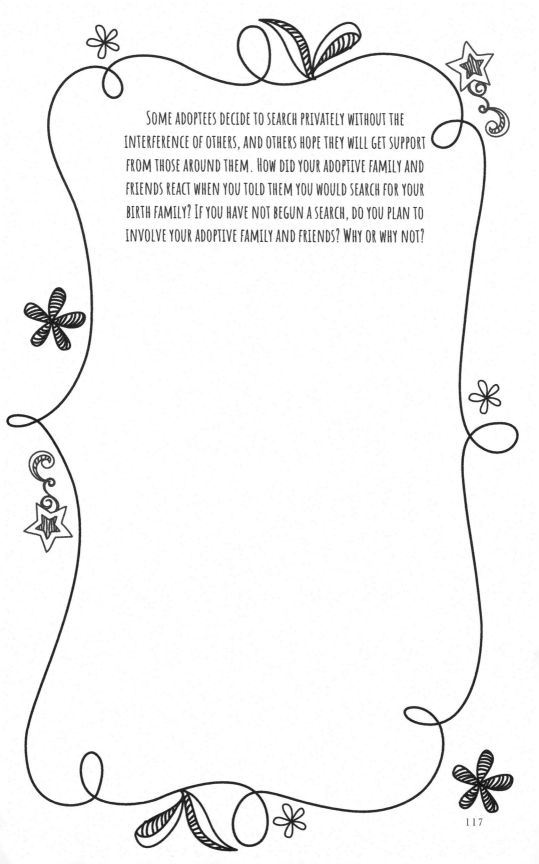

Some adoptees decide to search privately without the interference of others, and others hope they will get support from those around them. How did your adoptive family and friends react when you told them you would search for your birth family? If you have not begun a search, do you plan to involve your adoptive family and friends? Why or why not?

"Genes are like
the story, and
DNA is the
language that
the story is
written in."

Sam Kean

DNA TESTING HAS BECOME QUITE POPULAR TODAY AND ACCESSIBLE TO MANY PEOPLE. EVEN WHEN OUR BIRTH FAMILIES WITHHOLD INFORMATION, WE CAN ALWAYS RELY ON DNA. HAVE YOU EVER TESTED YOUR DNA TO FIND A BIRTH RELATIVE? WHAT DID YOU LEARN FROM YOUR DNA RESULTS? DID IT PROVIDE YOU WITH ANY TYPE OF CLOSURE? IF YOU HAVE NOT TESTED YOUR DNA, DO YOU PLAN ON GETTING YOUR DNA TESTED IN THE FUTURE? WHY OR WHY NOT?

"i feel like i'm stuck between two worlds wanting to be a part of the new but feeling at home in the old, now i'm not a part of either and i'm alone and lonely stuck in nothing."

Unknown

Sometimes I feel like I do not fit in my adoptive family. Even after reunion many adoptees discover too much time has passed to truly fit in with their birth family. Do you ever feel that way? Have you ever felt caught in between your adoptive family and your birth family? How do you balance having two sets of families?

"In all of us there is a hunger, marrow deep, to know our heritage— to know who we are and where we came from. Without this enriching knowledge, there is a hollow yearning. No matter what our attainments in life, there is still a vacuum, an emptiness, and the most disquieting loneliness."

Alex Haley

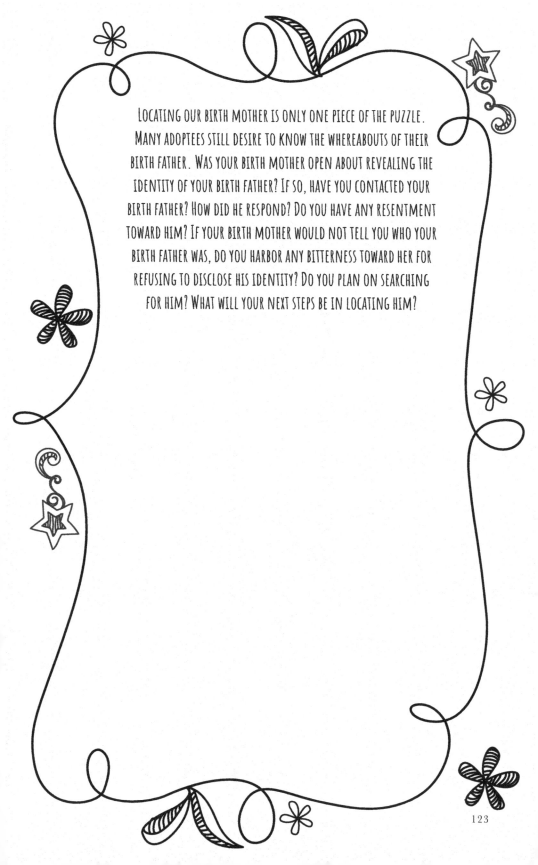

Locating our birth mother is only one piece of the puzzle. Many adoptees still desire to know the whereabouts of their birth father. Was your birth mother open about revealing the identity of your birth father? If so, have you contacted your birth father? How did he respond? Do you have any resentment toward him? If your birth mother would not tell you who your birth father was, do you harbor any bitterness toward her for refusing to disclose his identity? Do you plan on searching for him? What will your next steps be in locating him?

"A name
represents
identity, a deep
feeling and holds
tremendous
significance to
its owner."

Rachel Ingber

Many adoptees were named by their birth mother and renamed later by their adoptive parents. Sometimes the first-time adoptees discover their birth name is during a search. Our names tell us a lot about who we are; they are part of our identity. Look up the meaning of both names. Compare and contrast the meaning of your birth name and your adoptive name. Do you prefer one name over the other? Why or why not? If you do not know your birth name, do you feel like your adoptive name suites you?

Breathe Deeply

Today I feel... _____

because... _____

Self-care means taking care of yourself physically, mentally, spiritually, emotionally, and socially. Incorporating coping skills into your daily routine is one way to help maintain your mental well-being.

COPING SKILLS IDEA: INDULGE IN YOUR FAVORITE DESSERT.

Hydrate Often, Sleep Well, Eat Healthy

What can I do to take care of myself today?

_____

3 things that made me smile today:

_____

_____

_____

I Am Not My Experience

Today I am thankful for...

_____

Color the picture on the next page.

Personal Growth

"You can only
see a different
perspective if you
put yourself in
someone else's
shoes. Only then
can you learn
compassion.
Only then we
can start helping
each other."

Sef Azure

You are a well-known author, and the protagonist of your next book is a woman looking for a child she placed for adoption. Describe your main character. How old is she? What does she look like? What is her background story? What is her personality? Does she reunite with her child? If so, what happens when she does? How does it feel to put yourself in the shoes of a birth mother?

"Compassion is
to look beyond
your own pain,
to see the pain
of others."

Yasmin Mogahed

Have you ever had anyone show you compassion? What does the word compassion mean to you? In what ways can we show compassion for those who hurt us? Is there anyone in your adoptive or birth family for whom you do not have compassion? Why or why not?

"Healing doesn't
mean the damage
never existed.
It means the
damage no
longer controls
your life."

Akshay Dubey

Have you ever had to write or send a difficult letter? Maybe you were ending a toxic relationship, or you were saying goodbye to an old friend. Imagine sending a breakup letter to your adoption trauma. Tell it how much it hurt you. Tell it how much it will no longer control your life. Tell it that you are moving toward a place of healing and no longer want to see it again.

Dear Adoption Trauma,

"In order to love
who you are, you
cannot hate the
experiences that
shaped you."

Andrea Dykstra

Often when we go through some of life's greatest hardships, it makes us stronger than we ever realized we were capable of being. Adoptees are some of the strongest and most resilient people I know. Do you feel like adoption has strengthened your ability to build resilience? Why or why not?

"Sometimes it's
the journey
that teaches
you a lot about
your destination."

Drake

Searching for your birth family can be an emotionally exhausting process. It may send you into a tizzy of emotions that you never knew existed. You may have reunited with your birth family, or you may still be in the middle of a grueling search. No matter what happens, it is not your fault. This journey has made you confident, fearless, and even more resilient than you could ever have imagined, and this lifelong adventure is not over yet. You have come so far and will continue to go even further. In the process of searching for our birth families, often we end up learning a lot more about ourselves. What has your adoption experience taught you about yourself and life?

"I learned a long
time ago the
wisest thing i
can do is be on
my own side,
be an advocate
for myself and
others like me."

Maya Angelou

IN WHAT WAYS CAN YOUR USE YOUR ADOPTION EXPERIENCE TO ADVOCATE
FOR YOURSELF AND FUTURE GENERATIONS OF OTHER ADOPTEES?

Breathe Deeply

Today I feel..._____

because..._____

Self-care means taking care of yourself physically, mentally, spiritually, emotionally, and socially. Incorporating coping skills into your daily routine is one way to help maintain your mental well-being.

COPING SKILLS IDEA: PLAY YOUR FAVORITE SONG AND DANCE.

Hydrate Often, Sleep Well, Eat Healthy

What can I do to take care of myself today?

_____

3 things that made me smile today:

_____

_____

_____

I Am Not My Experience

Today I am thankful for...

_____

On the next page, create a list of your future goals then color the picture.

Conclusion

ongratulations! You have made your way through the *Rooted in Adoption Journal*. This is a huge step, and you should be proud. As you continue your adoption journey, you can visit old journal prompts to reflect on your growth and progress. Healing takes time, so I continually remind you to be kind, gentle, and patient with yourself. You matter, and your voice will help change the world.